D0122282

T O Y O U R *S*U C C E S S.

Thoughts to Give Wings to Your Work and Your Dreams

COMPILED BY DAN ZADRA

❖

DESIGNED BY
KOBI YAMADA AND STEVE POTTER

COM·PEŃ·DI·UM
INCORPORATED

PUBLISHING & COMMUNICATIONS

ACKNOWLEDGEMENTS

THESE QUOTATIONS WERE GATHERED LOVINGLY BUT UNSCIENTIFICALLY OVER SEVERAL YEARS AND/OR CONTRIBUTED BY MANY FRIENDS AND CLIENTS. SOME ARRIVED—AND SURVIVED IN OUR FILES—ON SCRAPS OF PAPER AND MAY THEREFORE BE IMPERFECTLY WORDED OR ATTRIBUTED. TO THE AUTHORS, CONTRIBUTORS AND ORIGINAL SOURCES, MY THANKS, AND WHERE APPROPRIATE, OUR APOLOGIES. –DAN ZADRA

WITH SPECIAL THANKS TO

JOHN APPLEGATE, GERRY BAIRD, NEIL BEATON, HAL BELMONT, BETTY BENDER, BETH BINGHAM, CHUCK CARLSON, DOUG CRUICKSHANK, JIM DARRAGH, JOSIE AND ROB ESTES, BILL GAGE, MARILYN GREY, JENNIFER HURWITZ, DICK KAMM, BETH KEANE, KAREN LAMB, LIAM LAVERY, CONNIE MCMARTIN, TERI O'BRIEN, VINCE PFAFF, JANET POTTER & FAMILY, DIANE ROGER, ROBERT & VAL YAMADA, TOTE YAMADA, ANNIE ZADRA, ARLINE ZADRA, AUGUST ZADRA.

CREDITS

COMPILED BY DAN ZADRA.
DESIGNED BY KOBI YAMADA AND STEVE POTTER.

PRINTED IN HONG KONG

CONTENTS

Dream

Hopes, Dreams and Possibilities
❖ Visions, Goals and Plans ❖
Imagination, Creativity and Innovation

6

Team

Collaboration, Teamwork and Leadership
❖ Loyalty, Synergy and Friendship ❖
Communication, Cooperation and Coordination

36

Care

Pride, Passion and Commitment
❖ Quality, Integrity and Service ❖
Values, Expectations and Standards

66

Dare

Confidence, Courage and Tenacity
❖ Choices, Decisions and Action ❖
Freedom, Opportunity and Fulfillment

96

A Gift to Inspire and Celebrate Your Achievements

*C*hances are you received this little book from someone who believes in you or appreciates what you do.

"I believe in you. I appreciate what you do. Here's to your success." Sincerely offered by the right person at the right time, the simplest words can often mean the most to us.

Take these words: dream, team, care, dare. Or these: integrity, craftsmanship, quality, responsibility, courage, faith, imagination, tenacity. If you place a high value on these simple terms, you will find–as I have–that the men and women quoted in this book are kindred spirits.

Compiling these great quotations for you has been a terrific experience. I realized once again that some of the most powerful, timeless and

useful ideas are also the shortest. "God bless America" is just three words, but three are all that's required. Shakespeare's "To thine own self be true" is just six words, but those six could make a life. The Lord's Prayer has 71 words; the Gettysburg Address has 271; the Ten Commandments have 297; the marriage vow just two.

The thoughts in this book average fewer than 35 words, and each is sincerely dedicated to your success. May this book become a source of inspiration and joy for you—just as your own work, dreams and accomplishments are an inspiration to others.

Dan Zadra

For my hero, Augie Zadra

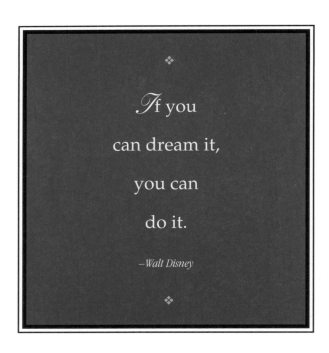

If you

can dream it,

you can

do it.

–Walt Disney

T O   Y O U R   *S* U C C E S S

❖

Every candle ever lit; every home,

bridge, cathedral or city ever built;

every act of human kindness,

discovery, daring, artistry or

advancement started first in

someone's imagination, and

then worked its way out.

You have that power—use it.

*I*f you do not think
about the future, you cannot have one.

—John Gale

———❖———

*I*f you don't have a dream, how can you have a
dream come true?

—Faye LaPointe

———❖———

*Y*our past is not your potential.
In any hour you can choose
to liberate the future.

—Marilyn Ferguson

*I*f you keep doing
what you've always done, you'll keep getting
what you've always got.

–Peter Francisco

❖

*M*an is the only animal
that laughs and weeps, for he is the only
animal that is struck with the difference
between what things are, and what
they ought to be.

–William Hazlitt

*D*reams come a size too big
so that we can grow into them.

—Josie Bisset

———— ❖ ————

*F*ar away there in the sunshine
are my highest aspirations. I may not reach them,
but I can look up and see their beauty, believe in
them, and try to follow where they lead.

—Louisa May Alcott

I like the dreams of the future
better than the history of the past.

–*Thomas Jefferson*

————— ❖ —————

To look up with unquenchable faith
in something ever more about to be. That is what
any person can do, and be great.

–*Zane Grey*

Dream™

*H*umanity cannot forget its dreamers;
it cannot let their ideals fade and die;
it knows them as the realities which it shall
one day see and know.

–James Allen

❖

*M*y interest is in
the future, because I am going to
spend the rest of my life there.

–Charles F. Kettering

Dream™

*T*he greatest achievement
was at first and for a time a dream.
The oak sleeps in the acorn;
the bird waits in the egg; and in the highest
vision of the soul a waking angel stirs.

–William James

— ❖ —

*Y*our hopes, dreams and
aspirations are legitimate. They are trying
to take you airborne, above the clouds, above
the storms–if you will only let them.

–Dan Zadra

*L*ife is a series of collisions
with the future; it is not the sum of what we
have been, but what we yearn to be.

–Jose Ortega y Gasset

———— ❖ ————

*W*hen one door closes, another opens;
but we often look so long and so regretfully upon
the closed door that we do not see the one
which has opened for us.

–Alexander Graham Bell

*L*ord, grant that I may always
desire more than I can accomplish.

–Michelangelo

— ❖ —

*W*hen dreams die, life is a
broken-winged bird that cannot fly.

–Langston Hughes

— ❖ —

*W*hen you're through changing,
you're through.

–Bruce Barton

TO YOUR *S*UCCESS™

I had no ambition to make a fortune.
Mere money-making has never been my goal.
I had an ambition to build.

–John D. Rockefeller

———— ❖ ————

*S*ome men march to the beat
of a different drummer, and some polka.

–Anonymous

———— ❖ ————

*T*wo men look through the self-same bars;
one sees mud, and one sees the stars.

–Frederick Langbridge

Dream

*D*reams are renewable.
No matter what your age or condition,
there are still untapped possibilities within you
and new beauty waiting to be born.

–Dr. Dale E. Turner

—— ❖ ——

*T*he greatest thing
in this world is not so much where we stand,
as in what direction we are moving.

–Goethe

*E*xtraordinary people visualize not
what is possible or probable, but rather what is
impossible. And by visualizing the impossible,
they begin to see it as possible.

–Cherie Carter-Scott

———— ❖ ————

*S*ome men see things as they are
and ask, "why?" I dream things that
never were and ask, "why not?"

–George Bernard Shaw

*S*et your sights high, the higher the better.
Expect the most wonderful things to happen, not
in the future, but right now. Realize that
nothing is too good.

–Eileen Caddy

— ❖ —

*W*hen we set exciting worthwhile goals
for ourselves, they work in two ways: We work
on them, and they work on us.

–EDGE Learning

*K*eep a daily diary
of your dreams, goals and accomplishments.
If your life is worth living,
it's worth recording.

–Marilyn Grey

❖

*W*ritten goals have a way
of transforming wishes into wants; can'ts into
cans; dreams into plans; and plans into reality.
Don't just think it–ink it!

–Dan Zadra

*D*on't pray for dreams
equal to your powers. Pray for powers
equal to your dreams.

–Michael Nolan

— ❖ —

*Y*our imagination can focus on
ugliness, distress and failure, or it can picture
beauty, success, desired results. You decide
how you want your imagination
to serve you.

–Philip Conley

If we wish to make a new world,
we have the material handy. The first one, too,
was made out of chaos.

–Robert Quillen

—— ❖ ——

You do not need to know how
you're actually going to achieve a goal when
you set it. Just repeatedly visualize the desired
result, and the "how" will open up to you.

–Vince Pfaff

Dream

Dream lofty dreams, and as you dream,
so shall you become. Your vision is the promise
of what you shall one day be.

–James Allen

—❖—

The future is of our own making–
and the most striking characteristic of this
century is just that development.

–Joseph Conrad

$\mathscr{T}$he first and most
important thing about goals
is having one.

–Geoffrey Abert

— ❖ —

$\mathscr{T}$he future never just happened. It was created.

–Will and Ariel Durant

— ❖ —

$\mathscr{Y}$ou cannot take charge
of the present if you are busy reliving
the setbacks of the past.

–Newman & Berkowitz

*G*reat minds
have purposes; others have wishes.

–Washington Irving

❖

*I*f you built castles
in the air, your work need not be lost;
that is where they should be. Now put
foundations under them.

–Henry D. Thoreau

*T*hose who dream by night awake to find
that it was vanity. But the dreamers of day are
dangerous; they may act out their dreams
with open eyes to make it possible.

–T. E. Lawrence

— ❖ —

*Y*ou have brains in your head,
and feet in your shoes. You can steer yourself
any direction you choose.

–Dr. Seuss

Dream™

*R*each beyond your grasp.
Your goals should be grand enough
to get the best of you.

–Teilhard de Chardin

❖

*T*hroughout the centuries
there were men who took first steps
down new roads armed with nothing
but their own vision.

–Ayn Rand

*G*enius seems to be
the faculty of having faith in everything,
especially oneself.

–Arthur Stringer

— ❖ —

*I*magination is
the beginning of creation. We imagine what
we desire; we will what we imagine; and at last
we create what we will.

–George Bernard Shaw

A genius is a person
who aims at something no one else
can see and hits it.

–Ervin L. Glaspy

— ❖ —

I shut my eyes in order to see.

–Paul Gaugin

— ❖ —

*T*he innovator is
not an opponent of the old, he is
a proponent of the new.

–Lyle E. Schaller

*D*iscovery is seeing what everybody else has
seen, and thinking what nobody else has thought.

–Albert Szent-Gyorgi

— ❖ —

*T*ake out your brain and jump on it–
it gets all caked up.

–Mark Twain

— ❖ —

*T*o stay ahead, you must have
your next idea waiting in the wings.

–Rosabeth Moss Kanter

Dream™

Choose to live, work and succeed
in the most powerful nation on earth:
Imagination.

–Dan Zadra

Imagination is more important
than knowledge.

–Albert Einstein

Often you just have to rely on your intuition.

–William Gates, Microsoft

TO YOUR *Success*™

*J*ust think of something that everyone
agrees would be "wonderful" if it were only
"possible." Then set out to make it possible.

—Armand Hammer

— ❖ —

A No. 2 pencil and a dream can take you
anywhere.

—J. Meyers

— ❖ —

*K*eep one still, secret spot where dreams may
go and, sheltered so, may thrive and grow.

—Children's rhyme

_S_orrow looks back.
Worry looks around. Faith looks ahead.

—*Beatrice Fallon*

— ❖ —

_Y_ou can't help getting older, but you don't
have to get old. New dreams, new works in progress—
that's the ticket for a long and happy ride.

—*George Burns*

— ❖ —

_N_ever fear the space between your dreams
and reality. If you can dream it, you can make it so.

—*Belva Davis*

*E*very thought is a seed.
If you plant crab apples, don't count
on harvesting Golden Delicious.

–Bill Meyer

———❖———

*T*o make a prairie
it takes a clover and one bee.
One clover, and a bee, and reverie.
And reverie alone will do,
if bees are few.

–Emily Dickinson

*M*oney never starts an idea;
it is the idea that starts the money.

–W. J. Cameron

❖

*W*hatever you're ready for is ready for you.

–Mark Victor Hansen

❖

*H*ats off to the past.
Coats off to the future!

–American Proverb

❖

No matter what

great things you

accomplish,

somebody helps you.

—Wilma Rudolph

❖

TO YOUR *Success*

❖

No one goes alone to the heights of

excellence. Whether your business

is building a loving family, a great

idea, a meaningful career, a work

of art, or a vast commercial empire,

your success will depend on others,

and theirs will depend on you.

*Y*ou can dream, create,
design, and build the most wonderful
idea in the world, but it requires people
to make the dream a reality.

–Walt Disney

———— ❖ ————

*A*nything one person can imagine,
other people can make real.

–Jules Verne

*A*mericans will reach the moon by standing
on each other's shoulders.

–John F. Kennedy

— ❖ —

*N*o one can whistle a symphony.
It takes an orchestra to play it.

–H. E. Luccock

— ❖ —

*P*roblems can become opportunities when the
right people come together.

–Robert Redford

Team™

*N*one of us is as smart as all of us.

–*Ken Blanchard*

— ❖ —

*W*inners can tell you where they are going,
what they plan to do along the way and who will
be sharing the adventure with them.

–*Denis Waitley*

— ❖ —

*W*orking together works.

–*Dr. Rob Gilbert*

Every great pitcher needs a great catcher.

–Casey Stengel

— ❖ —

Search for eagles and then teach
them to fly in formation.

–D. Wayne Calloway

— ❖ —

There is greatness all around you–
welcome it! It is easy to be great when
you get around great people.

–Bob Richards

*W*e have to be able to
count on each other doing what
we have agreed to do.

–Phil Crosby

———— ❖ ————

*Y*ou can work miracles
by having faith in others. To get the best out
of people, choose to think and *believe*
the best about them.

–Bob Moawad

*N*othing binds us one to the other
like a promise kept. Nothing divides us
like a promise broken.

–Mass Mutual

— ❖ —

*T*o promote cooperation and teamwork,
remember: People tend to resist that which is
forced upon them. People tend to support that
which they help to create.

–Vince Pfaff

Team™

*A*sk your team–they know the answer.

–Chuck Carlson

—❖—

*N*ever kill an idea, just deflect it.

–3M Slogan

—❖—

*T*his is a team effort. If you can't
put people up, please don't put them down.

–NASA slogan

Team™

$\mathcal{I}$'m just a country plowhand,
but I've learned to get a team beating with one
heart: If anything goes bad, I did it. If anything
goes semi-good, we did it. If anything goes
real good, they did it.

—Paul "Bear" Bryant

— ❖ —

$\mathcal{T}$he best leaders are very often
the best listeners. They have an open mind.
They are not interested in having their own way
but in finding the best way.

—Wilfred Peterson

TO YOUR $\mathcal{S}$UCCESS™

45

*E*ither we're pulling together,
or we're pulling apart. There's really
no in-between.

–B.J. Marshall

——— ❖ ———

*I*f you're too busy to help those
around you succeed, you're too busy.

–Bob Moawad

——— ❖ ———

*T*he best minute you spend
is the one you invest in people.

–Blanchard and Johnson

*M*otivation is everything.
You can do the work of two people,
but you can't *be* two people. Instead, you have to
inspire the next guy down the line to get him
to inspire *his* people.

–Lee Iacocca

——— ❖ ———

*T*here is a place for everyone in the
big picture. To turn your back on any one
person, for whatever reason, is to run the risk of
losing the central piece of your jigsaw puzzle.

–James St. Lyon

*I*t's a fine thing to have ability,
but the ability to discover ability in others
is the true test.

—*Elbert Hubbard*

— ❖ —

*T*here is no exercise better for the heart
than reaching down and lifting people up.

—*John A. Holmes*

— ❖ —

*T*hose who are lifting the world
upward and onward are those who
encourage more than criticize.

—*Elizabeth Harrison.*

If he works for you, you work for him.

–Japanese proverb

*L*eave no one out of the big picture.
Involve everyone in everything of any
consequence to all of you.

–Tom Peters

*M*arch in right now and clear the air.

–United Technologies

*H*elp each other be right,
not wrong. Look for ways to make
new ideas work, not for reasons they won't.
Do everything with enthusiasm,
it's contagious.

—Ian Percy

———— ❖ ————

*T*rust each other again and again.
When the trust level gets high enough,
people transcend apparent limits, discovering
new and awesome abilities for which
they were previously unaware.

—David Armistead

*L*eadership is action, not position.

–Donald H. McGannon

❖

*T*here are no passengers on Spaceship Earth.
Everybody's crew.

–Marshall McLuhan

❖

*T*here is something that is
much more scarce, something rarer than ability.
It is the ability to recognize ability.

–Robert Half

*T*eamwork is
less "ego" and more "we go."

–Brian Biro

❖

*T*he great companies and teams
are those that celebrate the differences.
They seek harmony not uniformity. They hire
talent not color. They strive for
oneness not sameness.

–Gil Atkinson

A team can win with almost
any offense, provided everyone on the team
is playing the *same* offense.

–John Wooden

— ❖ —

*M*ountain climbers always help each other.

–Tenzing Norgay, sherpa

— ❖ —

*T*he best thing to
hold onto in life is each other.

–Anne Zadra

If you want help, help others.
If you want trust, trust others. If you want love,
give it away. If you want friends, be one. If you
want a great team, be a great teammate.
That's how it works.

–Dan Zadra

——— ❖ ———

Life and business
are like the car pool lane. The best way
to reach your destination quickly is
to take some people with you.

–Pete Ward

*E*xcellence is what you
and your people create on your turf.
It can be done and it is done. There is no
excuse for not getting on with it
among your people.

–Tom Peters

— ❖ —

*T*here are two ways of exerting
one's strength–one is pushing down,
and the other is pulling up.

–Booker T. Washington

*M*ost of us, swimming
against the tides of troubles the world
knows nothing about, need only a bit of praise or
encouragement–and we'll make the goal.

–J.P. Fleishman

— ❖ —

*W*e could all take a lesson
from the great northern geese which
fly thousands of miles in perfect formation.
Formation flying is 70 percent more
efficient than flying alone.

–Dan Zadra

*G*reat discoveries and achievements
invariably involve the cooperation of many minds.

–Alexander Graham Bell

—— ❖ ——

*P*rogress is 95 percent
routine teamwork. The other 5 percent
relies on restless, inner-directed people who are
willing to upset our apple cart with
new and better ideas.

–Michael LeBoeuf

*T*he secret is
to work less as individuals and more
as a team. As a coach, I play not my eleven best,
but my best eleven.

–Knute Rockne

— ❖ —

*W*here all think alike,
no one thinks very much.

–Walter Lippmann

*I*t is not fair to ask of others
what you are not willing to do yourself.

–Eleanor Roosevelt

———— ❖ ————

*O*ne step by 100 persons
is better than 100 steps by one person.

–Koichi Tsukamoto

———— ❖ ————

*R*emember the law of
accumulation: The sum of many little
collaborative efforts isn't little.

–Michael Nolan

Team™

$\mathcal{G}$ive all the credit away.

–John Wooden

———— ❖ ————

$\mathcal{T}$he main ingredient
in stardom is the rest of the team.

–John Wooden

———— ❖ ————

$\mathcal{T}$he only sacred cow
in an organization is its principles.

–Buck Rodgers, IBM

*T*he greatest thing you can do
for any individual or any group in your day
is to help them find the best.

–Katherine Logan

— ❖ —

*T*he real winners in life
are the people who look at every situtation
with an expectation that they can make
it work or make it better.

–Barbara Pletcher

*D*o good things for others and people
may accuse you of selfish motives.
Do good anyway.

—*Dillon Laughton*

———❖———

*D*on't over-react to the trouble makers.

—*Warren Bennis*

———❖———

*T*here are no exceptions to the rule that
everybody likes to be an exception to the rule.

—*Malcolm Forbes*

*I*t's easier for people to see it
your way if you first see it their way.

—*Jack Kaine*

———❖———

*W*e must learn to lift as we climb.

—*Angela Davis*

———❖———

*T*he two kinds of people
on earth that I mean
Are the people who lift and
the people who lean.

—*Ella Wheeler Wilcox*

*A*ny manager who can't
get along with a .400 hitter is crazy.

–Joe McCarthy

— ❖ —

*I*n the heroic organizations,
people mentor each other unselfishly.

–Don Galer

— ❖ —

*T*he best team doesn't win
nearly as often as the team that
gets along best.

–Dr. Rob Gilbert

*C*elebrate what you want to see more of.

–Tom Peters

— ❖ —

*C*ould a greater miracle take place
than for us to look through each other's
eyes for an instant?

–Henry David Thoreau

— ❖ —

*B*e kind to one another.

–Jim Henson, Sesame Street

Give the world

the best that you have,

and the best will come

back to you.

—*Madeline Bridges*

TO YOUR *Success*

❖

No calling on earth is insignificant

if it is accomplished with pride

and artistry. Do whatever your heart

leads you to do, but do it so well

that those who come to see you do

it will bring others to watch you

do it again and again and again.

*I*f you love what you do,
you will never work another day in your life.

–Confucious

——— ❖ ———

*T*he more you love what you are doing,
the more successful it will be for you.

–Jerry Gillies

——— ❖ ———

*T*o love what you do and feel that it matters–
how could anything be more fun?

–Katharine Graham

If you are working on something
exciting that you really care about, you don't have
to be pushed. The vision *pulls* you.

–Stephen Jobs

— ❖ —

There's no grander sight in the world
than that of a person fired with a great purpose,
dominated by one unwavering aim.

–Orison Swett Marden

— ❖ —

To make a living is no longer enough.
Work also has to make a life.

–Peter Drucker

*H*e who has a 'why'
to live for can bear almost any 'how.'

–Nietzsche

— ❖ —

*G*ood work is never done in cold blood;
heat is needed to forge anything. Every great
achievement is the story of a flaming heart.

–A.C. Carlson

— ❖ —

*I*f a man hasn't discovered something
that he will die for, he isn't fit to live.

–Martin Luther King, Jr.

Care

*C*are enough for a result,
and you will almost certainly attain it.

–William James

———❖———

*N*ever let what you
cannot do interfere with what you *can* do.

–John Wooden

———❖———

*T*alent is what you possess;
genius is what possesses you.

–Malcolm Crowley

Care™

*L*ife is no brief candle to me.
It is a sort of splendid torch which
I have got hold of for the moment, and I want to
make it burn as brightly as possible before
handing it on to future generations.

–George Bernard Shaw

— ❖ —

*L*ive your life so that your children
can tell their children that you not only
stood for something wonderful–
you acted on it.

–Dan Zadra

TO YOUR *S*UCCESS™

72

*N*obody grows old merely
by living a number of years. We grow old
by deserting our ideals. Years may wrinkle
the skin, but to give up enthusiasm
wrinkles the soul.

–Samuel Ullman

———❖———

*W*hen we do the best we can,
we never know what miracle is wrought
in our life, or in the life of another.

–Helen Keller

*D*on't care what others think
of what you do; but care very much about
what you think you do.

–St. Frances DeSales

— ❖ —

*L*ife owes us little; we owe
it everything. The only true happiness
comes from squandering ourselves
for a purpose.

–John Marm Brown

*I*ntegrity is what we do,
what we say, and what we say we do.

–Don Galer

— ❖ —

*P*eople don't really care
how much you know until they know
how much you care.

–Mike McNight

— ❖ —

*T*here is no such thing
as a minor lapse of integrity.

–Tom Peters

*O*ne person *can* make
a difference and every person should try.

–John F. Kennedy

———❖———

*T*he lure of the distant and the
difficult is deceptive. The great opportunity
is where you are.

–John Burroughs

———❖———

*T*he place you are in
needs you today.

–Katharine Logan

Good ideas are not adopted
automatically. They must be driven into
practice with courageous patience.

–Admiral Hyman Rickover

———— ❖ ————

Some succeed because they are
destined to; most succeed because
they are determined to.

–Anatole France

*A*ct as if what you do
makes a difference. It does.

–William James

— ❖ —

*L*et me tell you the secret
that has led me to my goal. My strength
lies solely in my tenacity.

–Louis Pasteur

— ❖ —

*T*here is no failure
except in no longer trying.

–Elbert Hubbard

*M*ost people never run
far enough on their first wind to find out
they've got a second. Give your dreams all you've
got and you'll be amazed at the energy
that comes out of you.

–William James

———— ❖ ————

*T*onight, when you lay your head
on your pillow, forget how far you still
have to go. Look instead at how far
you've already come.

–Bob Moawad

*I*t's a funny thing about life.
If you refuse to accept anything but the best,
you very often get it.

–Somerset Maugham

— ❖ —

*W*hen you get right down to the root
of the meaning of the word "succeed," you find it
simply means to follow through.

–F. W. Nichol

*D*o what you can,
with what you have, where you are.

–Theodore Roosevelt

—— ❖ ——

*O*ne person with a belief is equal
to a force of ninety-nine who have only interests.

–John Stuart Hill

—— ❖ ——

*T*here is no traffic jam
on the extra mile.

–Business axiom

God will not look you over
for medals, degrees or diplomas,
but for scars.

–Elbert Hubbard

— ❖ —

There is no finish line.

–Nike Motto

— ❖ —

Those who stand
for nothing may fall for anything.

–Alexander Hamilton

It's easy to have faith in yourself
when you're a winner, when you're number one.
What you've got to have is faith in yourself
when you're not a winner.

–Vince Lombardi

— ❖ —

*P*rogress results only from the fact
that there are some men and women who refuse
to believe that what they know to be right
cannot be done.

–Russell Davenport

*A*nybody can come up with new ideas.
What's in short supply are innovative people–
persistent mavericks who believe so strongly
in an idea, they will do whatever it takes
to make it a working reality.

–Michael LeBoeuf

——— ❖ ———

*I*t's important to take pride
in what you do or what you stand for.
The kind of pride I'm talking about is not the
arrogant puffed-up kind; it's just the whole idea
of caring–fiercely caring.

–Red Auerbach

$\mathcal{E}$nthusiasm is contagious. Start an epidemic.

–Don Ward

— ❖ —

$\mathcal{T}$he best part of one's life
is the working part, the creative part.
Believe me, I love to succeed; but the real
spiritual and emotional excitement
is in the doing.

–Garson Kanin

— ❖ —

$\mathcal{Y}$ou can outdo you–if you really want to.

–Paul Harvey

*A*ge puzzles me. I thought it was
a quiet time. My seventies were interesting and
fairly serene, but my eighties are passionate.
I grow more intense as I age.

–Florida Scott-Maxwell

— ❖ —

*T*he fight is won or lost far away
from witnesses–behind the lines, in the gym
and out there on the road, long before
I dance under those lights.

–Muhammad Ali

As you get older, don't slow down.
Speed up. There's less time left.

–Malcolm Forbes

— ❖ —

It's what we learn
after we know it all that counts.

–A. C. Carlson

— ❖ —

Throw your heart over the bars
and your body will follow.

–Veteran trapeze performer

I must not rust.

–Clara Barton

— ❖ —

*W*hich of you is going
to step up and put me out to pasture?

–John Wayne

— ❖ —

*Y*ou may occasionally
give out–but never give up.

–Mary Crowley

Care™

*B*lessed are those
who expect nothing, for they shall
not be disappointed.

–Jonathan Swift

———— ❖ ————

*Q*uality never goes out of style.

–Levi Strauss

———— ❖ ————

*S*chool is never out for the pro.

–Jim Williamson

*G*ood enough never is.

–Debbi Fields

— ❖ —

*I*n communities where men build
ships for their own sons to fish or fight from,
quality is never a problem.

–J. Deville

— ❖ —

*W*hen your heart is in your dream,
no request is too extreme.

–Jiminy Cricket

*P*eople don't give a hoot
about who made the original whatzit. They want
to know who makes the best one.

–Howard W. Newton

— ❖ —

*T*he greatest crime in the world
is not developing your potential. When you do
what you do best, you are helping others.

–Roger Williams

*T*he road to success has
many tempting parking places.

—*Steve Potter*

❖

*T*he winds blow strongest
against those who stand tallest.

—*F.C. Hayes*

❖

*P*repare. The time to win your
battle is before it starts.

—*Frederick W. Lewis*

*Quitting is a permanent solution
to a temporary situation.*

—*Dr. Rob Gilbert*

— ❖ —

*Success requires three bones—
wishbone, backbone and funnybone.*

—*Kobi Yamada*

— ❖ —

*Take your job seriously
but learn to laugh at yourself.*

—*Don Ward*

*E*nthusiasm is faith set on fire.

–George Adams

———— ❖ ————

*F*ormula for success:
Underpromise and overdeliver.

–Tom Peters

———— ❖ ————

*W*hen the one Great Scorer comes
to write against your name, He marks–
not that you won or lost–but how
you played the game.

–Grantland Rice

Care™

*I*f you consistently do your best,
the worst will never happen.

–B. C. Forbes

❖

*L*uck is earned. Luck is working
so hard at your craft, service or enterprise that
sooner or later you get a break.

–Paul Hawken

❖

*T*he real friend of his country is the person
who believes in excellence, seeks for it, fights
for it, defends it, and tries to produce it.

–Morley Callaghan

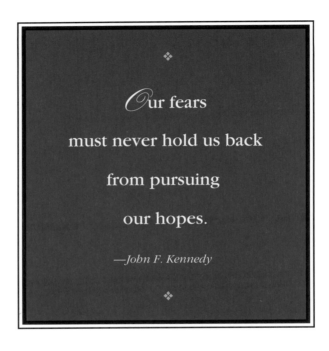

Our fears

must never hold us back

from pursuing

our hopes.

—*John F. Kennedy*

TO YOUR *Success.*

❖

There has been a calculated risk

in every stage of American

development—pioneers who

were unafraid of the wilderness,

scientists who were unafraid of the truth,

businessmen who were unafraid of failure,

dreamers who were unafraid of action.

A great pleasure in life
is doing what people say you cannot do.

–Walter Gagehot

———— ❖ ————

*A*nything I've ever done that ultimately
was worthwhile…initially scared me to death.

–Betty Bender

———— ❖ ————

*T*he first and great
commandment is, never let them scare you.

–Elmer Davis

Dare™

*T*ake a chance!
All life is a chance. The person who
goes farthest is generally the one who is
willing to do and dare. The 'sure thing'
boat never gets far from shore.

–Dale Carnegie

———— ❖ ————

*T*ake risks.
You can't fall off the bottom.

–Barbara Proctor

Dare™

*T*he moment you commit and quit
holding back, all sorts of unforeseen incidents,
meetings and material assistance will rise up to
help you. The simple act of commitment is a
powerful magnet for help.

–Napoleon Hill

— ❖ —

*Y*ou can either take action,
or you can hang back and hope for
a miracle. Miracles are great, but they
are so unpredictable.

–Peter Drucker

*P*eople will try to tell you that all
the great opportunities have been snapped up.
In reality, the world changes every second,
blowing new opportunities in all
directions, including yours.

–Ken Hakuta

— ❖ —

*T*o get profit without risk,
experience without danger, and reward
without work, is as impossible as it is to
live without being born.

–A. P. Gouthey

Dare

*A*nyone with a new idea
is a crank–until the idea succeeds.

–Mark Twain

— ❖ —

*T*he biggest things are often
the easiest to do because there is
so little competition.

–William Van Horne

— ❖ —

*W*herever you see a
successful business, someone once made
a courageous decision.

–Peter Drucker

TO YOUR *S*UCCESS™

102

*I*t's a good idea
not to major in minor things.

–Anthony Robbins

❖

*S*ome things arrive in their own
mysterious hour, on their own terms and not
yours, to be seized or relinquished forever.

–Gail Godwin

❖

*T*he Wright Brothers flew
right through the smoke screen of impossibility.

–Charles F. Kettering

Dare

$\mathscr{A}$ll the beautiful sentiments in the
world weigh less than a single lovely action.

–James Russell Lowell

———— ❖ ————

$\mathscr{O}$nly begin and then the mind grows heated;
only begin and the task will be completed.

–Goethe

———— ❖ ————

$\mathscr{O}$ur duty is to proceed
as if limits to our ability do not exist.

–Teilhard de Chardin

*A*las, for those who never sing,
but die with all their music in them.

—*Oliver Wendall Holmes, Jr.*

— ❖ —

*N*o, you never get any fun
out of the things you haven't done.

—*Ogden Nash*

— ❖ —

*P*eople who never
get carried away should be.

—*Malcolm Forbes*

$\mathscr{A}$ll humanity is divided into three classes:
those who are immovable, those who are movable
and those who move!

–Benjamin Franklin

——— ❖ ———

$\mathscr{L}$ife is like a tiger.
You can either lie down and let it lay
its paw on your head–or you can sit
on its back and ride it.

–Ride The Wild Tiger

*A*rgue for your limitations
and, sure enough, they're yours.

–Richard Bach

— ❖ —

*D*o the thing and you will have the power.

–Emerson

— ❖ —

*O*thers can stop you temporarily;
only you can do it permanently.

–Don Ward

*A*s you grow older,
you'll find the only things you regret are
the things you didn't do.

–Zachary Scott

— ❖ —

*S*it, walk or run, but don't wobble.

–Zen

— ❖ —

*T*rust your crazy ideas.

–Dan Zadra

I cannot give you
the formula for success, but I can
give you the formula for failure–which is:
Try to please everybody.

–H.B. Swope

— ❖ —

*P*ay no attention to what
the critics say; no statue has ever been
erected to a critic.

–Jean Sibelius

A good plan vigorously executed
right now is far better than a perfect plan
executed next week.

–General George Patton

——— ❖ ———

*T*here are risks and costs
to a program of action–but they are far less
than the long-range risks and costs
of comfortable inaction.

–John F. Kennedy

*A*ction is eloquence.

–Shakespeare

— ❖ —

*B*uild it and they will come!

–Field of Dreams

— ❖ —

*I*f we did all the things
we are capable of, we would literally
astound ourselves.

–Thomas Edison

*O*ur doubts are traitors,
and make us lose the good we oft might
win by fearing the attempt.

–Shakespeare

———— ❖ ————

*T*wo roads diverged in a wood,
and I–I took the one less travelled by, and
that has made all the difference.

–Robert Frost

$\mathcal{D}$on't be afraid to take
a big step if one is indicated. You can't cross
a chasm in two small jumps.

–David Lloyd George

——— ❖ ———

$\mathcal{I}$t is not because things are difficult
that we do not dare; it is because we do not
dare that things are difficult.

–Seneca

*F*or every obstacle
there is a solution—over, under,
around or through.

–Dan Zadra

— ❖ —

*P*ick battles big enough
to matter, small enough to win.

–Jonathan Kozol

— ❖ —

*Y*ou have to think anyway,
so why not think big?

–Donald Trump

Form the habit of saying
"Yes" to a good idea. Then write down all
the reasons why it will work. There will always
be plenty of people around you to tell you
why it *won't* work.

–Gil Atkinson

— ❖ —

You know far more than
you know you know. Never ask, "Can I do this?"
Ask instead, "*How* can I do this?"

–Dan Zadra

$\mathscr{C}$hances are, the more puzzled looks
your idea creates, the better your idea is.

–United Technologies

———— ❖ ————

$\mathscr{L}$ive all you can; it's a mistake not to.

–Henry James

———— ❖ ————

$\mathscr{U}$se the word "impossible" with
the greatest caution.

–Werner von Braun

*H*igh achievers spot rich opportunities
swiftly, make big decisions quickly, and move into
action immediately. Follow these principles and
you can make your dreams come true.

–*Dr. Robert Schuller*

— ❖ —

*Y*ou can't leave footprints
in the sands of time if you're sitting on your butt.
And who wants to leave buttprints in
the sands of time?

–*Bob Moawad*

*C*ause something to happen.

–Paul "Bear" Bryant

———— ❖ ————

*I*t's amazing what ordinary people can do
if they set out without preconceived notions.

–Charles F. Kettering

———— ❖ ————

*Y*ou can't build a reputation
on things you are *going* to do.

–Henry Ford

TO YOUR *S*UCCESS™

I believe that genius is an
infinite capacity for taking life by the
scruff of the neck.

–Christopher Quill

— ❖ —

*T*he world is an oyster, but
you don't crack it open on a mattress.

–Arthur Miller

— ❖ —

*T*here is only one you.
God wanted you to be you. Don't you dare change
just because you're outnumbered!

–Charles Swindoll

*A*nything is possible.
Nothing is too good to be true.

–*Kobi Yamada*

— ❖ —

*N*othing splendid has ever
been achieved except by those who dared
believe that something inside them was
superior to circumstances.

–*Bruce Barton*

A year from now
you may wish you had started today.

–Karen Lamb

— ❖ —

*A*ll things come to those who go after them.

–B.J. Marshall

— ❖ —

*L*et us go, now, and wake up our luck.

–Cyprian proverb

$\mathcal{D}$on't bunt. Aim out of the ballpark.

–David Ogilvie

— ❖ —

$\mathcal{T}$here is no security on this earth.
Only opportunity.

–Douglas MacArthur

— ❖ —

$\mathcal{W}$hy go into something to test the waters?
Go into it to make waves.

–Michael Nolan

*W*henever the human adventure
reaches great and complete expression,
we can be sure it is because someone has
dared to be his unaverage self.

–Rae Noel

——— ❖ ———

*Y*ou are one of a kind; therefore,
no one can really predict to what heights you
might soar. Even you will not know
until you spread your wings!

–Gil Atkinson

If you risk nothing,
then you risk everything.

—Geena Davis

— ❖ —

The future is not a gift, it is an achievement.

—Henry Lauder

— ❖ —

If you're already walking
on thin ice, you might as well dance.

—Gil Atkinson

*W*e must have courage to bet
on our ideas, to take the calculated risk,
and to act. Everyday living requires courage if life
is to be effective and bring happiness.

–Maxwell Maltz

———— ❖ ————

*A*nd will you succeed?
Yes indeed, yes indeed! Ninety-eight and
three-quarters percent guaranteed!

–Dr. Seuss

*T*he only safe ship in a storm
is leader*ship*.

—*Faye Wattleton*

——— ❖ ———

*N*ever let anyone monkey with your swing.

—*Mickey Mantle*

——— ❖ ———

*A*mateurs hope.
Professionals make it happen.

—*Garson Kanin*

*N*o matter what the statistics say,
there's always a way.

—*Bernard Siegel*

— ❖ —

*N*ever mistake motion for action.

—*Ernest Hemingway*

— ❖ —

*T*here can be no progress unless
people have faith in tomorrow.

—*John F. Kennedy*

Also available from Compendium Publishing are these spirited
and compelling companion books of great quotations.

Because of You™
Celebrating the Difference You Make™

Brilliance™
Uncommon Voices From Uncommon Women™

Forever Remembered™
A Gift for the Grieving Heart.™

I Believe in You™
To your heart, your dream and the difference you make.

Little Miracles™
To renew your dreams, lift your spirits, and strengthen your resolve.™

Reach for the Stars™
Give up the Good to Go for the Great.™

Thank You™
In appreciation of you, and all that you do.™

Together We Can™
Celebrating the Power of a Team and a Dream.™

Whatever It Takes™
Thoughts to Inspire and Celebrate Your Commitment to Excellence™

You've Got a Friend™
Thoughts to Celebrate the Joy of Friendship™

These books may be ordered directly from the publisher (800) 914-3327.
But please try your bookstore first!
www.compendiuminc.com